CW01501818

Sophie Dumont is a poet and copywriter based in Bristol and Bath. Her poetry won the Brian Dempsey Memorial Prize and has appeared in *The Rialto*, *Magma*, *The Moth*, *Ink Sweat* and *Tears and Mslexia* among others. Dumont has an MA in Creative Writing from Bath Spa University and has held writing residencies along Bristol Harbourside with Boat Poets and Exeter Quay through Literature Works.

Sculling

Sophie
Dumont

corsair poetry

CORSAIR

First published in the United Kingdom in 2025 by Corsair

1 3 5 7 9 10 8 6 4 2

A CIP catalogue record for this book
is available from the British Library.

ISBN: 978-1-4721-5995-3

Typeset in Perpetua by M Rules
Printed and bound in Great Britain by Clays Ltd, Elcograf S.p.A.

Papers used by Corsair are from well-managed forests
and other responsible sources.

MIX
Paper | Supporting
responsible forestry
FSC® C104740

Corsair
An imprint of
Little, Brown Book Group
Carmelite House
50 Victoria Embankment
London EC4Y 0DZ

The authorised representative
in the EEA is
Hachette Ireland
8 Castlecourt Centre
Dublin 15, D15 XTP3, Ireland
(email: info@hbgi.ie)

An Hachette UK Company
www.hachette.co.uk

www.littlebrown.co.uk

for Wiz

Contents

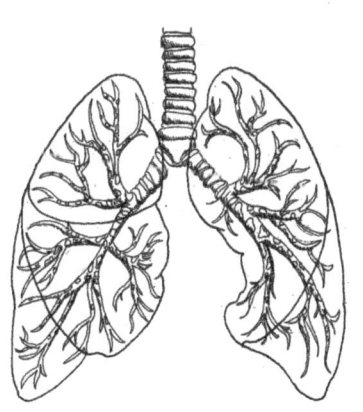

To Kayak

To be driven forward when sitting still
To kayak (verb) and *kayak* (noun)
To doodle the outline of your boat, the shape of closed lips
To butterbur, balsam, to adder's-tongue
To walk past white water five years from now
      and instinctively seek your line
To use *swim* as an insult, a sign of mistake, as in, *Did you swim today?*
To have a latex neck and wrists
To be guided by the moon-silver underleaf of mugwort on the bank
To be an angler's nemesis
To Teifi, to Wye, to Usk
To seek the playground of a weir or chute
To hide from your mum the deep scratch along the crown of your helmet
      where river turned you upside down, backed you into a corner,
      reminding you how low and dark its voice can go
To pillwort, fen violet, valerian
To neoprene
To spend all afternoon digging water a shade lighter than mud
To know a town from the echo of its bridges
To be driven, damp, hungry, back to your starting point

The Curse

On my sixteenth birthday I trained to be a Canoe Coach, which meant I was briefly the youngest Canoe Coach in Britain. I soon realised the club was a sanctuary for the cursed or the about-to-be-cursed. When we returned each week to the black box of the boathouse the woman with the dog named Afon had fresh cuts. The stitch-dots either side told us of the evenings she'd felt herself too deeply. One man broke both his legs, crushed when his boat's nose tipped over a weir. He relied on the same boat to move, to feel wind. Another drowned. Each week I watched my coach ceremoniously tie our boats to the roof of the van, watched him thread the evening through a carabiner and fasten it down with his weight. We grew into each other for three years. He died at twenty by aquaplaning into a tree and I left the club. I separated myself from my neoprene skin and the reddish-black closed eyelids of underwater. I have a new weekly routine. On Tuesdays I stand naked in front of the mirror by the window and watch the evening cast its scars.

Monday Is Ochre

You left on a Monday,
now Monday is when I have to breathe the most,
when the thing I can't swallow is at its thickest,
like the earth we used to roll between our fingers.
We were potters given too many flowers,
couldn't fire vessels quick enough to hold them.

Here is an X-ray of me on Mondays, a tree in winter,
bird's nest lodged between the branches,
between the veins, between my throat and my words.

Since I heard you leave,
I sing in a different octave. I've stopped working with clay.
There are six days still left in this week.
Your pigment is under my fingernails.

Observations of Air

In the late sun's pollen soup, I took my niece and two Magnums to the park to watch hot-air balloons rise. We sat on the dry grass beside the red lake of nylon. It rippled like bedlinen from the whip of a fist over an unmade bed, like parachute games when I was her age and the way I'd trap a pocket of air to watch it roll to the shore of someone else.

We worked on our ice cream, our tongues growing pale and numb. Industrial fans chewed through the evening. She spotted another balloon three clouds away and another a city away from that. She pointed at the furthest one. *Baby billoo*, she said, pinching it out with finger and thumb because all her objects are measured by Mummy, Daddy and Baby.

When the bulbous red was about to take flight, I was down to the wooden peg of my ice cream. In silence, a gap formed between earth and basket. I felt the trees root deeper. We waved at sky-borne strangers who disappeared behind an oak then reappeared on our drive home. To her, they'll never land. They'll simply be in and out of her moment.

Now, I glance at her in the rear-view mirror. By the time we're home the grass marks on the backs of our thighs will have gone. She'll be snoring hot air from the soft O of her lips.

Notes on Hung Road

— It's not a working dock anymore.

— A girl is propped on a mother's hip. Mother has bent knees
to steady herself at centre of boat like mast.

— I miss your skin.

— Someone comments on skipper's signature being illegible.
Being wave-like. She's been on water too long.

— I phone you. Tell you I want to get excited by this city.
Want to understand the rain's inclination to its gutters.

— I fall in love with the word *silt*, which is so similar to spilt
or tilt or guilt, which are all forms of mistake.

— You haven't phoned back. You won't trade Aire
for Avon – yet. I wear 'yet' like a lifejacket.

— As we exit Avon's mouth, Wales reveals her shoulders.
We turn back.

— There is a pipeline from Avonmouth to Heathrow carrying
aviation fluid.

— Not a working dock anymore?

— The grass turns to smooth sand on the riverbank
   the way the hair stops at my ankles.

— Mast-mother points to ghost ships, repeats fact that boats
   were tied to branches to avoid hulls tipping at low tide.
   Skipper says it would have looked like a fleet hanging
   from the trees. Called Hung Road.

— Dock not working.

— Sometimes I take a picture of myself after I cry. Proof?

— As we step off boat, our backs are told the masts of SS Great
   Britain are named after days of the week.

— A crane lifts two men in a box above the ship.
   They set to work repairing Thursday.

Outfitting a Kayak

My second-hand *Dagger* is moored in the town hall.
Today I am making it fit like a limb. I sit in the cockpit,
rocking gently on the lino floor.

I cut a hunk of foam with scissors from the first aid kit,
wedge padding between my hip
and the boat's bones.

I consider the kayak's origin, built to hunt seals, whale,
polar bear. How the Inuit mould a boat to its builder,
measure it against their anatomy:

Length: three spans of the builder's outstretched arms.
Width: the builder's hips, a fist either side.
Depth: a fist and outstretched thumb.

Wives stitch sealskin, stretch it over a whalebone frame.
I fill the gap between knee and cockpit's coaming.
I lose where skin ends and boat begins.

I replace lino for Avon's bank. I hip-shuffle off the edge,
nose-slice into river, bounce, pull with my paddle
to steady and settle with the closeness of water.

Few Inuit ever learn to swim. The sea is grave-cold,
they know the way a whale's ribcage can cradle a body,
lung-like, to keep it afloat.

I don't believe in ghosts

                              but take a sandwich up to one every day,
take it away again uneaten. In the attic Grandad lies,
refuses to wash, eat, take his pills, his body forgetting itself
with every unswallowed mouthful.

While we do things alive people do, we hear his footsteps,
the shuck-shucking of his slippers, wearing himself away.
He tells the carer he has three grandchildren.
We bet on which of us he'll be getting rid of next.

We listen to the ceiling. He's sitting in the armchair under
the skylight. He waits. We all wait. We hope for the sound
of running water from the bathroom, as if Grandad might wash
off Grandad and quicken the whole bleak process of dying.
Grandad draining out. Grandad in the pipes,
but the bathroom is bone-dry with the lack of Grandad.

To escape his stale-scented non-being, I walk. I pass a pool
of crocuses the same diameter as the bare tree above,
as if the tree had dropped its purple in favour of winter clouds.
I'll climb upstairs to check on him when I get back,
hope to open the door and find only sky.

Abecedarius for the
World's First Named Heatwave

Zoe arrived in the shape of a bag of tricks
you left behind the mirror. After Zoe, it'll be Yago,
Xenia, Wenceslao, then Vega – all giving wildfires
wilder tongues. Zoe translates to *Life*, to *Eve* who wears
V-necks and sliders because someone has to be
used as an answer when Facebook shares dog paws
too blistered to stand on concrete. Zoe has us
shade-hopping in the shadows of people we can't name,
reveals bones of missing daughters in dried lakes,
questions our part, points to the matches in our hand.
Pure hot-blooded body, I cross a bridge last walked
over in the seventies. It was at the bottom of a reservoir
now an unknown village we can forget by blinking.
Milk turns too soon, the tap runs at mouth temperature.
Lying in separate rooms, we spread our limbs,
kept sedentary with wet towels on our stomachs. Zoe
jinxes us from the inside out while fruit flies bloom.
I enter a supermarket for ice, move down aisles
holding my arms up to the air-con as Zoe searches my
ghost. I reach for the freezer with blackberry-stained
fingertips but ice is out of stock. Ankles thick with living,
evening still 29 degrees. Behind front doors,
decay quickens, news repeats: *human bodies rely on
cooler nights to recover from day.* We wake to pull

blinds down, to hide from Zoe's glare. We want her
absence, or for her to come softer, without a name.

Teaching a T Rescue

First, capsize your kayak, replace sky with riverbed.

Once upside down, rapidly learn a new sense of black.
Reach for your hips.

Bang the hull three times, raise birds. Swing your arms
bow to stern like walking swiftly underwater

until you feel another boat's nose. The rescuer will butt
their bow to your centre weight, creating a T.

Find their boat's handle, hold it with both hands. Hip-
flick to rotate your boat upright. All force from the hip.

It's tempting to pull with your arms, to taste air sooner.
This won't work. The pendulum

of your head will swing you back into river. But hip-flick,
and your upper body will follow.

Your head must be the last part to surface.

Simulation

The signal announces the waves.
A pink and pocked crowd flocks to the main pool
and begins its wading.

The blue's frequency accelerates.
Each swell carries heads and arms and hair
like kelp. They all face the back wall

as if in their desire to be moved
it will open up to reveal the origin;
the shipwreck, the pulsing sky, the rain
giving wet another texture.

A boy throws himself into the crest of the storm
while a girl holds up her hand, waving
to show her mother how much she loves drowning.

Permission

Terrier-training, you'd wait on the curb
until she obeyed. Across the road, I stood as bait.
She'd twist, bolt onto hind legs before the whip-tug
of her collar and your Bristolian lilt: *Heel, Heel*.
I watched your command, the taut lead slackening
with submission. Your rod-straight back,
army haircut the colour of wet sand.

You'd just finished college, spent summer
with your pack of boys: Splinter, Gobbo, Tyson, Ellis.
All chasing your tails, your banter bounding
through the city, eyes like overturned soil, wanting.
You'd spark campfires on the cliff edge,
Suspension Bridge flexing, mighty, in front of you,
reaching across the gorge.

This morning I'm curled in bed with my now-
elderly dog yipping and running in her dreams.
I wonder if she remembers your scent – the cloud
of Calvin Klein you'd walk into, over-washed polo shirts.
Days like this my stomach is a coiled spring.
I zip myself up, set out on the walk. We wait
on the curb for your permission, for the release: *Go on*.

Mugwort

Artemis vulgaris or Wise Woman's Power Plant

Named after the goddess of the moon,
lobed and weakly hairy, we find it
clinging to a bank of the Frome.

With finger and thumb, I turn its green
like a page, show you the silver
of its underleaf. I scrape my nail along

to inspect the tinder of tiny white hairs.
From our book, we know it repels moths,
sleeplessness, evil, but I am drawn

to how it can shift a woman's cycle.
Steep it in tea or tuck it under your pillow
to wake up heavy and thrumming,

bedsheets flecked with the red relief
of a late menstruation.
We bought seeds out of some kind of homage

to choice, to power over the body, planted
in pots lining our city terrace in spring –
our own pagan ring of protection.

We sit in the centre, our sacred space,
free of dependents. Our arm hairs rise
to evening as it widens with song.

That night, I dream of them fully grown,
swaying skyward. Each leaf pierces night
when June wind lifts, carries moonlight.

girl as half-chewed light

when looking into the closed poem of this window a girl in lit class
acts bored to be cool like nothing's being thought but awareness of
how her body is positioned / her glossy hair angled to reflect / other
girls aren't sure whether to hate her or dream of her one quick glance
/ their own breath left on the glass of her / she gives herself the choice
of packed lunch in the loo or on the way home because there's vul-
nerability in eating / everything sticks to lip gloss and cling-wrapped
sandwiches are embarrassing / better still bin the lot / she walks
past the new glass building people are calling *sexy* because you can
either see through it or see yourself in it / am i a trick of the light yet
/ when was i supposed to want not leo's romeo or claire's juliet but
the fish tank between them / tell me what i should be / tell me what
you want to see because if i'm glass then i'm daughter of sand / tell
me *you're snatched* like the aim is to be taken without consent / did
you think that mirror was a window you could open / did you think
this warning was a poem / tell me again that compliment i like the
one that's shaped like an empty glass / *look at you* / *you're hardly there*

Adolescent

We take off our watches and melt,
lips first then limbs into limbs.
Foxes move moonlight with their screams,
the mole repositions his black,
and badgers press together,
speaking perfume.

Red on the white of my mattress,
spilt ink after a signature;
this is moving closer,
I stink of nearly adult.

My body's calendar strikes
like a gong on the nose of the month.
It is heavier since we melted.
In the bath my crimson swirls from me in plumes,
a subaquatic vapour merging with the water,
becoming inseparable.
I unplug the day but stand up too quick,
my adult left spinning.

Self-Portrait as Rain

It was raining when we buried you, when the seed potatoes weren't looking. It was rain that took your car's tyres, skimmed you through a puddle lit by moon and headlight then washed night over your upturned dead body in the upturned dead car until morning.

It was raining when you came to surprise me at my university halls, when I broke up with you and when two weeks later rain took you. I speak to you through river, through all water, because the gutters were full of you this morning and I mistook the spilling of water for your forgiveness.

It was raining when I walked home from town, the small of my back wet with sweat. At the bottom of the garden I stripped down to blue knickers, slid on the decking's algae to the edge of the koi carp pond, the edge of womanhood, and stepped in. I went back to my room and quietly drowned before being asked down for dinner.

It was raining that day in reception when I came in from play like a dog made wild. I cut chunks out of my hair with spring-assisted red scissors and was sent to the headmaster's office to explain myself.

It was raining when I jumped into the puddle as a small girl because it seemed as though the clouds were on the floor and I might just be able to jump into sky. Instead, sky ran down my shins and into my wellington boots to stain the soles of my white cotton socks grey.

That is to say, I enter rain to meet myself.

The Night Collector

My niece starts teething when the birdsong slows.
As she screams, the winter moon wills white
into her gums and won't let her sleep.

When my first milk tooth was yanked out by a toffee eclair
I pretended I believed in the tooth fairy,
just to receive her letter.

I wanted to see how small my dad could write, to file
his words on a letter the size of a closed mouth.
He told me it's possible for a third set to push for light.

I dream of a woman's grave. *Buried with a new set of teeth*
is carved in cursive under her name.
I see the nodules of my spine at night, heaping

mud into her grave, over the skull I somehow know
is mine, but that third set of teeth is licked-plate white,
and the mud slides off them again and again.

I wake in sweat, tonguing my gums.
All night I clench my bright miniature headstones.
I am not ready for that final set to rise.

My own daughter hasn't met me.
How small I can write? How much of myself can I fold
in half and half again to slide below her moon-white pillow?

Orbit

for Nan

To remove your cataracts, cuts were made,
a needle or a small pair of forceps used
and the milk-like protein sucked out.

I saw a time-lapse of the sky, clouds
inhaled by something over the horizon.

You relied on years of muscle memory
to know the right height of the keyhole
at your rib, the light switch at your shoulder.
The house was your anatomy.

Your eyelids never fully closed when you slept.
Too soon after you were given sight
you passed in your sleep, your eyes two slivers of sky.

Bath at 4.46 a.m., Mid-June

The milkman nods. His van tends to the crescent. Three streets away a suitcase chatters over cobbles. The reared claw of a digger. Newspapers gifted in twine on shop doormats. A portrait of a missing cat lifting from a lamppost. The scent of croissants, fresh bread, butter. A coat draped over railings by its hood, full and round in the wind. The absurd chortle of a seagull as it mates with another silhouetted on a roof. The angle of one window catches the tipping sun, as if the room is on fire. White tulips wait.

The Five Stages of Grief

It's January all month when I prune the apple tree,
portion myself into the cutlery drawer.

I scrape my thumbnail around the Sellotape wheel
in search of the thin edge.

All night the white rabbit searches for the top hat
it jumped from, but the hat is just a hole so I usher
the rabbit to its grave.

My head is an empty cinema.

Women are born with all their eggs inside their ovaries.
I was born with all my possible daughters.

instinct of a glass eel

i have not known wet motive like this
            butter-knife-blunt
sliver of want
            a comma of pinbones
white truths
            tell me again what category of god
is carried four thousand miles
            on the gulf stream
to arrive as a mirror
            then slip up the spine of a city
to turn elver then yellow
            then silver then stay deceiving
the reeds upstream
            to be on the red list
deftly under the guise
            of trickster renting
in the house of river
            sleep in the day on its back
play dead then eat the dead
            then look sky dead in the eye
to writhe in its own mystery
            before the siren of sargasso
calls the body back
            but before turning on its slick axis
after twenty years moving uphill

like a secret spilling over and over
it edges a moon-blue field in somerset
            wriggling with its own sharp hunger
butts its nose against the bank
            uses its squit-slate body of desire
to pierce the film of night
            heave itself out and begin to climb

Object Permanence

A butter-bell chuckle is followed by a *peekaboo*
and in a hilarious, exhausting game of disappearing
and appearing, you become a person.

I take away the blue scissors
that you were exploring with your tongue
and pop them in the drawer.

Last week, this wouldn't have mattered to you – no,
not *mattered*, I mean registered
as loss. Like a bird's brief black across a window.

Today, you release a murderous note,
dangle your weight from the drawer handle.
I am watching you learn grief.
Empty-handed, I'm mourning the girl of last week.

On Pigeons

The pigeons in St Mark's Square, Venice, are the same as the pigeons sitting on the head of King George in Trafalgar Square, are the same as the pigeons hiding in the Dark Arches under Leeds train station. They are the same as the pigeons outside my front door, which I watched pick at a polystyrene takeaway box when you walked out for the second time and I became familiar with the back of you.

The pigeons here in Gundulić Square, Dubrovnik, listen for the bell of noon and appear in their hundreds from behind terracotta. They shoot up into a fierce blue and begin their tilting of the sky, like the holographic postcards my nan sent us, or when you'd tilt a shiny object to project light somewhere else.

Three locals have emptied a swathe of seeds at the centre of the market. They sit on a trolley to watch the tornado dive. The dark pile is three birds thick and moving like water over rocks. Customers cover their mouths with napkins, with corners of clothing as the ruffle and violence whips up under-wing soot. The white dirt hovers on light like August snow.

I walk away, pushing my nephew you've never met. I swig water and the cold dislodges something in my throat. Soot. Snow. Something that's been carried in flight and then I think about eating pigeon meat, and I wonder where that strange energy goes, whether we hold flight in our stomach for a day or so and then I think that this is what   is, a kind of translation (after digestion) into flight.

First Date

Always in cheap candlelight,
I ask their middle name, darkly,
with eye contact that could drop a bird.
Maybe I ask for it as a shortcut to the soft
flesh of this evening, maybe to pocket it,
keep it cold in the glove compartment
or on a carabiner clip with the spare names.
Maybe I'm asking after the woman
you came from, what she wanted to hide.
Maybe I want you to think I want your core.
Tell me. Tell me you don't have one.

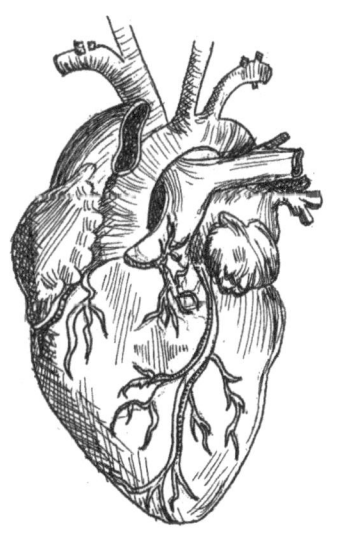

Notes addressed to the person
who received my ex's heart

— You take a pill every day to prevent your body
    from rejecting his heart.

— I dream you're in a hospital bed down the corridor,
    a hole in your chest. I'm at the side of T's bed,
    watching his death arrive for twelve hours.
    The doctor runs down the corridor with it dripping
    in their blue gloves.

— T's skin had the texture and weight of wax.

— Every hour his mum lifted the tube a little, coated
    his lips with Vaseline.

— A priest came, which felt like a joke.

— A relative I'd never met bought me tea in a polystyrene
    cup.

— Two weeks before this I had broken us up
    with the firm hand of *I've met someone else.*

— A nurse made me paint T's palm with green paint, press
    it on paper like a toddler's. I pushed each finger down

to make a print. I was dead myself when I did this.

— Someone took the paper somewhere.

— I imagined a room of colourful dying hands hung like
bunting.

— I don't remember the days after the decision was made to
switch T off. The week is white.

— In the dream the doctor trips, drops the heart. It skids
across the floor and leaves a red streak. A nurse wheels
over the heart with a trolley of clean tools and someone
else has to sweep it up with a dedicated dustpan and brush,
like in bar jobs where the yellow dustpan and brush is for
BROKEN GLASS ONLY.

— An ITV producer emailed me for pictures of T.
Father meets boy who received his son's heart. My mum
told me not to watch.

— I watched the programme with the lights off, my door
locked, pressing a bruise.

— I stared a hole through your khaki jumper, through
your starched shirt, right to T's/your heart.

— Nobody mentioned how that heart had been mine for
three years. This is a sickly-pink thought, I know, because
it's just a heart, as boringly everyday as waking up.

— My eyes were sore from watching your bright face.

— As I stared, I mouthed things I know your particular heart
  disagrees with:

> *Don't drink more than two coffees before breakfast*
> *Don't listen to the third track of Bon Iver's second album*
> *Don't run up Beechen Cliff*
> *Don't drive over to hers as a surprise*
> *Don't ask her what's the matter*
> *Don't let her sit a room away from you*
> *Don't let her open her awful young mouth*

Perennials in Bloom

Another record-breaking summer. I hide from it
during the day, go out in the evening when it's cool
to where Guilt glows below the wood pigeon's nest.

Yesterday, I dug up the wild Guilt that stole water from the apples,
found it breath-taking behind the house, its stem towering
above me, had me wincing at its fierce purple.

Into the night, I gathered and tied posies of it,
propagated from the Guilt I dropped in your grave,
the kind that twists and binds.

Sculling

You taught me how to scull in a kayak silently from one bank to the other, to do it with such efficiency that on your second glance I was sitting on a different river. You taught me how to lift my thigh to tilt the hull to allow the water to move under, whilst I moved over, to draw a figure of eight deep in the river with my paddle almost vertical. You taught me to watch the effect of my existence, watch the silt cloud like an explosion stilled underwater. You taught me to stir the Avon to move my body closer to yours.

Now, I am eight winters older, drawing that same figure of eight in the doodles that loop around the voice at the other end of a phone call, in the S of my signature that links my forename to my surname, in the ampersands I use instead of closing a sentence & then you weren't on the other side of the bank, and then there was no bank, and I'm sure it's muscle memory from the wrist's roll to index finger and thumb on pen because river and ink are the same consistency and I pull myself through something silently because it never stops or stops or stops

Universal Declaration of River Rights

Developed by the Earth Law Center in 2017

1. THE RIGHT TO FLOW
2. THE RIGHT TO PERFORM ESSENTIAL FUNCTIONS
   WITHIN ITS ECOSYSTEM
3. THE RIGHT TO BE FREE FROM POLLUTION
4. THE RIGHT TO FEED AND BE FED BY
   SUSTAINABLE AQUIFERS
5. THE RIGHT TO NATIVE BIODIVERSITY
6. THE RIGHT TO REGENERATION AND RESTORATION

Personhood

Since 2017, legal personhood status has been granted to the following rivers in order to give them rights: Atrato in Columbia, Ganges and Yamuna in India (overturned in 2018), Komi Memem or Laje in Brazil, Los Cedros in Equador, Mutuhekau or Magpie in Canada, Ouse in England, Whanganui in New Zealand and all rivers in Bangladesh.

I disappear myself down a ladder
into Avon, become downstream
movement, spin to full-lung float

on my back, the water within
my body only skin away from river,
which itself is organ-wet.

The sound of river is my blood
rushing to meet me. In swimming,
I add my self to river's, add my

heart to the hearts that river carries
and therefore has within it – the wet
slick beating of barbel, chub, eel.

River has the yellow eyes of heron,
lives the mayfly's day over and over
and over, speaks through the blue zip

of kingfisher. Its lungs are the pooled
air under a swift's wing, the loaming
of leaves mudding into silt,

the sweetness of pineapple weed
crushed underfoot on the bank.
River fills itself with its self,

ends at its mouth but speaks on
and up and through and with.
It is a holding and being held.

At the clump of reeds I turn,
begin the work of upstream,
limbs pulling against the second

most tidal river. I am shocked by
its strength, its proximity still
to its parents: Gravity and Weather.

All week river speaks
through the dull ache of my muscles –
a body reminding itself of its living.

A conversation had while the carrots grew deeper

Higher, higher, my nephew ordered on the bucket swings behind the allotments. The chains yawned with gravity's rust-red predictability. He reached up, fingers spread into suns. *You'll touch the clouds*, I said, wanting so much to give him that. He snapped his arms back, stuffed balled-up fists into his pockets. *No, they're ouchy clouds. Spicy. Hot.* Reaching for this poem, I probed him, *Oh, clouds are smoke?* He agreed worriedly. *Where from?* I asked. Silenced by the lulling of being swung, the clouds greyed his cold face. The wind nodded the pine branches along to my rocking back and forth like worship. *Something big, emptied.*

Night Paddle

Under an oak moon, a cold moon, a long night moon,
you and a friend went to the river with torches, slipped
your kayaks into black and cut between bloated banks.

When you returned alone in the pitch-small hours,
something in you had broken, your face the blue-white
of that moon. I was scared to ask what happened.
Ignorance might rewind the night, push it back upstream.

You stuttered that you felt him slip from your fingers,
wrenched by flood water. I can't imagine a blacker black
than underwater at night. River disguised its stones as stars,
pushed him in the direction of forever.

You folded me in half with your crying, knelt with your face
in my stomach while I scrambled to grow into adult hurting.
With both hands I held your head, moon-heavy, a life away.

Negative Space

I keep my Blu Tack in a plastic bag meant for sandwiches, or dog shit. I don't remember the last time I stuck up anything. I use it more as a stress-reliever, squeezing the putty so that it fills my fist. I put down the mass and it resembles the negative space within my balled-up palm. I drop it back into the bag to clench the next time, a slight difference in the imprint of each fist. My stress can be seen. It reminds me of the plaster they used to fill the holes in Pompeii. They took away the ash and found the cast of a human, its mouth open for flies.

Waiting for a Heart Transplant

Tonight Programme, ITV, November 2012

I'm desperate for a new heart,
but have come to terms with losing myself —
says the young man yet to receive your heart.

A surgeon states, *There's a shortage of hearts.*
We are all living longer. People aren't dying
in road accidents due to increased safety measures.

One month after this programme aired,
your car spun on a flooded road, crumpled
into a tree and enclosed you like a gift.

There's a 4 to 6-hour window for a heart to last
outside a body. To get to his body, your heart
travelled 110.3 miles in the fragile hours.

I imagine a bomber plane tearing across counties,
dodging the New Year fireworks.

It hovers over Watford, opens its belly
and the bomb of your heart plummets,
thuds wetly into the young man's chest.

Did I hear it?

So recently your chest
had been the seashell I pressed to my ear in bed.

Across the country, the first bright *beat*.

Three-Second Storm

In the brief black of passing under a bridge
the temperature drops, the sound alters
to something similar to a wild sea,
or the way a cloud's shadow burns a patch in a field,
the way I feel my name thrown in a conversation
in another city and the hairs at the base of my spine
rise to hear its significance.

The map shows another coming up to the left,
another momentary storm. We soak up the sky
while we can, turn, and watch the arch grow.
Then, we are in it. We are cold. Our hair lifts
and a boy in a red cap opens his throat, throws sound
into shadows, as we've all done,
in the reckless hope of its return.

Yarrow

Achillea millefolium: Named after Achilles of Greek myth, who used it to treat the wounds of soldiers, yarrow soothes skin and stems bleeding when crushed and applied.

On Father's Day, we picked yarrow —
feathery grey-green leaves under
a heavy head of terminal clusters.

Tiny bright flowers form a dome
the size of a cupped hand.
We pushed it into a milk bottle,
placed it at the centre of his table.

Helpless, we want the dementia
to show itself as a wound,
to see the blood of it, stem its spread.

As the petals dried and dropped
in white dust on the table,
something reached far back into him —

he spoke of a blue duffle coat
he had as a child, the itch of its hood,
the train set he got that Christmas,
how it snowed in clumps of white quiet.

His memory of this morning,
picking yarrow, is as thin as a petal –
a snowflake melting as it falls, and I am
the girl at the window, hoping it will settle.

Piano Ghost

The piano swung out from the room.
The cow-bulk of it groans from underneath
its overcoat of wrapping, loose enough
to not sweat and warp. The crane's claw hovers.
The piano's black belly eclipsed the morning.

During packing up the rest of the house
the grand was kept at 50% humidity, 65-78° F,
maintained like keeping a throat warm
as if preserving the bacteria of its last long hum.

A new tenant moved into the room
from which the piano had been removed.
Four coin-sized dips hold the eye's attention
where the feet left marks in the thick pile.

The tenant fills each print with ice cubes,
leaves them overnight. She dog-ears her page,
switches off her bedside lamp, imagining
the symphony of melting, the minor notes of water
expanding the space left by the weight of sound.

Advent

I opened the door of December 22nd, gave you its chocolate
to melt on your tongue. Your mum stopped buying you calendars
long before we found the adult in each other attractive.

We've known each other since the Tamagotchi ban,
since changing for PE in the same classroom, since our sex parts
were the smooth V of nothing, where Barbie and Ken's just end,

fall off into a gap of imagination. Now, you manage a club in town,
saving for London. I pretend I have a jumper in lost property at 3 a.m.,
wait for you to distribute the tips.

We hurry our clothes off on a childhood sofa. *You have arm hair now.*
You hollow out my face with your stare, as familiar as my own,
then full-name me like the register taken after a fire alarm.

You full-name me all the way into the New Year. I let you sleep.
In the morning, you thank me for being a reason to sleep.
Resolutions already thinning, you return my books unread.

Christmas trees appear outside front doors, laid on their sides –
the flat disc bottom of their trunks. I can barely smell the pine.
We walk through a forest only visible in its felling.

The Pillow

I was young and it was already too late,
when I realised my pillow had a pulse.
After milk, I laid down my head,
hair splayed like seaweed,
and the drumming began,
marching through dreams
towards my still body, half there.
A *ticker   ticker   tickering* from within.
I opened my pillow's lips.

Mum found me at dawn
sweat-drenched as though drowned,
the pillowcase ripped to a ribcage
where I'd spent the night searching
for the clock in each seam.

December Hangs Above Me to the Left

Sometimes I seek the nearest peak,
scale it until there's a cloud to look down on,
until my ears roar and the wind is all there is.
On my descent, I turn my head away
and in this disregard, I make silence.

Sometimes I think of December and get stuck

switching the light on and off,
and my room fills and empties, until it feels right,
until I allow myself to take my finger off the switch,
for a moment long enough to not control
the exhausting work of day and night.

Let me explain. December is the month I left you

and by the end of that month the rain had pooled
the roads into mirrors of black sky and your car skidded
into the nearest tree and the force ate your shoes,
the shoes I bought you at the beginning of December,
and you died in your socks.

You, as Gravity

Throwing and catching keys again and again,
you'd walk up the gravel driveway, grinning.

I'd already swung myself open, but you knew
of a second door, the one under my feet.

Index of Exeter Quay / From the blue door, I beckon

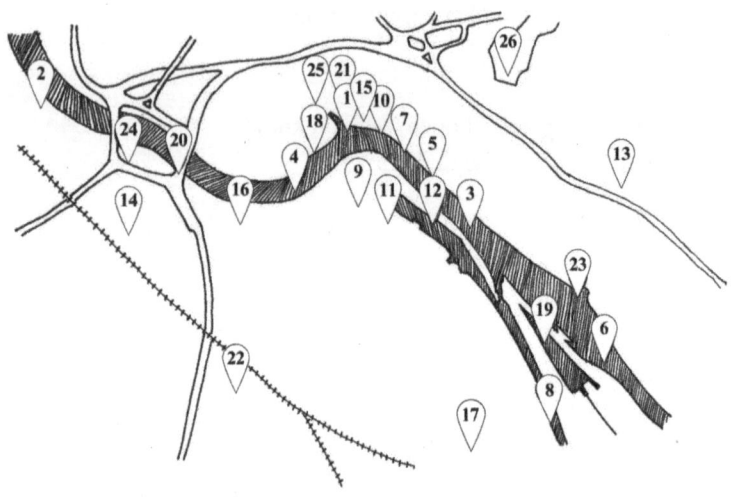

1. It's here that I first read: *Exeter is considered to have lost its route to the sea.*

2. A woman is wearing *The Great Wave off Kanagawa* as a mask over her mouth.

3. Kayakers dig all morning and leave no trace of what they've moved.

4. For *river,* see >> *mirror*

5. I bought a ceramic bowl, fired with a glass nugget within it to create the effect of a pool of water at its base.

6. There's a fire extinguisher lodged in the weir. See also *shoes, traffic cone, water's memory of moor*

7. It's the hottest summer on record and tap water is the same temperature as kissing. I return each week to the blue door of the Custom House, watch the mirage of this water.

8. I canoe to find Countess Wear, the suburb containing the weir built by the eighth Countess of Devon in 1284 to block Exeter's thriving port. No one knows where the weir is; the Exe swallowed it whole: an *archaeological dilemma*.

9. I replace my notebook with a sketchbook. I collage a river and use only ripped pieces of sky.

10. This porch was Elizabeth Dock four hundred years ago, used for small barges to offload larger ships too big to come into the wharf. The dock is now inland, is now an ice cream menu, a chiropractor with the original mooring rings on the shop's front.

   10.a. I remember sheltering under this canopy, 1 a.m., breathing vodka ghosts into the night, the club pulsing next door. The rain was so heavy it wiped each second clean. I stood on what I now know to have been river and pulled some-one in closer. The rain spilled down the stairs to meet us, returning to its former self as I lost mine.

11. Hulls: upturned palms, pockets, a middle name.

12. A group of girls in lifejackets crouch to touch the river, like a mother's hand gauging a forehead.

13. For *sisterhood*, stay here.

14. I read a tweet stating that house martins don't drink water off the ground – only that which is suspended.

15. A girl in my workshop tells me she will describe these windows as mouths.

16. *Ick* = river creek, cow creek, watering place.

17. *Black Thursday, 1960. So much rain it burst the banks and, for a brief period, Exeter was cut off from the country.* At what point does river become sea?

18. I've noticed the fierce heat has me speaking in eddies, in circling pools.

19. The spillway – a section built especially for the spilling.

20. My sister calls, holds the phone up to show me my five-year-old niece in an iridescent leotard. She has just learned to do a bridge at gymnastics. I hold my phone up so that my niece's body arches over the Exe.

21. I dunk my cookie into weak tea, notice the eels writhe in the cornicing.

22. *I remember walking home from school after the flood. The water was up to here.* She slides her hand under her chin – throat-height.

22.a.   *My mother nearly bought that house. There's a mark across the
wall where the river pushed itself against the sofa, licked at the
paintwork. You can't get a watermark out of plaster.*

23, 24, 25. (Buddleia)

26. I tell my brother of my recurring dream: I wake in a flooded
house. The moon has lit a path for the sea to rage up the spine
of the Exe. I walk slowly downstairs, returning myself with
each cold step. *River rises up me like it does the wall in a lock*, I say,
it rises up me like light.

Typographer in the Basement

When all out of words, I seek him. I watch him at work at the letter-press, the intent behind each letter. Each type is elongated for grip, like holding a comet's tail between index finger and thumb. He slots each one into the composing stick; his sentences begin upside down, right to left. I am seduced by the cases of keys tipped with symbols of punctuation. One case is labelled 'Furniture', and is full of white space the typographer handles, positions on the stone bed, filling the space around his words. I run my fingertips through the lead commas and then brush along the larger cherrywood letters. He unlocks the quoins that hold it all in position, allows his message to settle on a new surface. He warms the ink by smearing the black around the roller. Then, with a tender grasp, he turns the wheel. The impression is made. Neither of us have opened our mouths.

We Keep Our Chlamydia in a Bell Jar

You can buy anything on eBay. You can buy scaled-up soft toy versions of viral cells. So after we tested positive, we sat down for coffee and you presented me with the luminous green furball. I instinctively stroked our Chlamydia, looked into its eyes.

I kept our Chlamydia among the scatter cushions because that's where soft things go. Then my parents and the dog came to stay and I thought it might get dog-slobbered and dissected so you rolled it into the glass dish and placed the cloche on top, as if snuffing out a candle. A contemporary boat in a bottle, we placed it on the mantelpiece.

We speak of the Chlamydia but not the before. The green face sits in its museum, smiling, preserving our eighth hour together. At the end of our first date I entered your room like a ship and you shut the door, firmly and finally, on my wake.

Things Associated with You

You enter a room like a child
letting go of a balloon, red
as the open throat of a chick
in anticipation of being fed
which relates to sirens deep in a near city
like prayers thrown to the wind
and in turn the moment I walk behind a car
just as it pulls away and I'm left
to trace the curved outline of nothing
which reminds me of the words I push
in your mouth when we kiss
which corresponds to the indent in skin
left by the string of a helium balloon,
which is called *karelu*, in the language of Tulu

Grief Diary

By writing it down I'm killing you.
The first line of my first entry to my first love.
Someone had researched the words *grief* + *coping* + *strategy*
then handed nineteen-year-old me the black Moleskine.

Reading it back, my tense is all over the place –
language hadn't caught up, was still in bed with you.
There are different coloured pens for different coloured evenings
when I wrote things neither of us would have wanted:
I wish you got me pregnant before you went.

Yes, I'm shocked by that self
but I remember feeling a duty to carry you on,
and I remember crying as the nurse scratched out my implant –
'this might hurt a little' – and the last part of you exited my body.

I'm now a decade older than you ever were
and there is still so much left to kill.
I am considering the cost of life-ing a child, of making a feeling thing,
of digging a grave for the future.

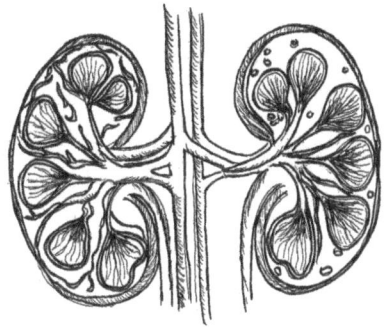

Water Act 1989

1. Anglian Water ~~Authority~~
2. Welsh Water ~~Authority~~
3. North West Water ~~Authority~~
4. Northumbrian Water ~~Authority~~
5. Severn Trent Water ~~Authority~~
6. Southern Water ~~Authority~~
7. South West Water ~~Authority~~
8. Thames Water ~~Authority~~
9. Wessex Water ~~Authority~~
10. Yorkshire Water ~~Authority~~

The Answer

Wessex Water was responsible for 43,931 sewage spillages in 2024. On average, 120.4 times a day. These lasted for 404,880 hours across 1,151 locations in their service area.

Data source: Environment Agency

When the urine infection moved uphill to my kidneys,
my body drank from a drip for 7 plastic days, pushed
8.5 jacket potatoes to my sister at the foot of the hospital bed.
Under strip lighting, nurses worked on E. coli in my blood.

Before this, the heat of my A Level summer thickened,
eddied in the drains, the backs of my knees. The next day still
wasn't results day. Rain's tiny mouths hadn't spoken
for weeks so I reached for it – the Avon – the answer
I refuse to stop asking for, an opening the shape of a river,
an entrance the shape of me.

Sisterhood

We are both five foot one and a half with the same blonde mass of matted hair, same birthday month, same split from our men in the week of January 4th. Before that, we both had a love who died before he reached twenty-two. Now we were moving out, to move in together.

We used our diary as wadding to pack up the kitchen. We ripped out a week of pages from the spine, layered personal goals between plates, stuffed past addresses in the gaps. We emptied December into a bell jar.

When we moved into the emptiness of the new home we lay on the carpet in our two rooms, as if making snow angels. Last week we were strangers and yet sometimes we look in a new mirror. We turned our head to the wall between us, felt the vibration of each other's voice in our palm and talked.

Alarm

In my first winter away from home, the sun didn't tip
over the windowsill to let me crawl out of my
blue-stuffed head. I lived with my light off,
didn't want other freshers to see the slit of awake under
my door, didn't want them to know I was busy emptying
myself of bile, flushing my ghosts again and again.

Sitting on the hard mattress, face lit by laptop,
I heard the squealing corridor of girls barrel to a foam party.
I called my mum, *I think I have Teenage Depression*
and before my next shower, she'd booked compassionate
leave; drove me to lectures and sat outside like a bodyguard
with coffee, told the sun to get its shit together.

I gave her my single bed, floated numb down the road
to slide next to a boy whose way of briefly taking me
out of myself had become addictive. In the morning,
Mum said the fire alarm had gone off in the early hours.
She'd had to single-file in the car park
in M&S nightie and cowboy boots.

Only in this poem have I thanked her
for standing there in my stead, breathing
into January's black song with a crowd of bleary kids,
announcing herself on the register as the mum of a daughter
lying in another bed in flames.

a simple guide to what happens

Found phrases from Devon tourism guides and signage around Exeter Quay

A guide to / prevent pollution / BACK FOR 2022 /
Wait for the falling / RIVERS / overwintering / in autumn
on their way back to West Africa / Watch out for / YOUR BOAT /
there are several slipways / reaching / wild / Be considerate of /
storytelling / in shallow depth / STAY / constantly changing /
This beautifully marked emerald-green dragonfly is one of the first
to emerge in early spring / it will / Share This Space /
with the / Hairy Dragonfly / Mussels / Lugworm / feeding on /
wonderland / Souvenirs

Do not climb the height of yourself for a better view

Do not place your beer bottle on the party's open windowsill
Do not wait for this man to stop talking about his appetite
Do not knock your bottle accidentally-on-purpose
Do not imagine it falling for decades through thick moonlight
Do not see yourself wearing bottle-green
as you're spun by this man who turned up late
Do not spend the evening wishing you'd moved across the room
to the swaying woman with a fleet of ships on the small of her back
Do not want to cling to the hull of her all night or later dream
of using her lustred mouth as a bowl to keep your songs
Do not think of the bottle   stopped
an inch before the pavement, an inch before smashing
into all the mirrors you've ever escaped

NO HEAVY PETTING

Every week the old man in speedos steadied himself against the wall at the exit of the family changing rooms, foot balanced across his knee, brushing sock fluff from in-between his toes. We'd wade past him, through the strip that separates the changing rooms from the swimming pool. The grim water oddly warm with bits in: floating plasters, a toe ring, a used verruca sock caught in a scrum-eddy. I'd wince through the purgatory, fiddling with my rubber locker-key wristband as it pulled at my baby hairs. Nan would make a beeline for the jacuzzi where I'd desperately try not to lock eyes or legs with the person opposite, while Nan's tits bubbled, her top-lip sweat adding to the stew. To avoid that, I'd get kicked in the back at the top of the tube slide by a boy too impatient for the green light. I'd head to the quiet deep end by the pool's filter that pushed out simulated waves. I'd twist my body against its desire to float, kick down to the bottom where the blue was richer and climb the horizontal grid like a ladder, pushing how long I could hold my breath, diving further into knowing myself, before coming up for air.

2020 / The Summer I Spoke in Quizzes

Round 39: General knowledge
I pour gin.

Round 27: Nature
There are dolphins in Venice's canals
and I have a crow in my bath.

A fly makes a halo above the bottle opener,
which hasn't been back in the drawer since spring.

I no longer know my height but I know an octopus
has three hearts, David Attenborough never learned
to drive and I am talking to flies.

Round 14: History
Shoes, belts, the pressure of a stranger's body.

On Thursdays at 8 p.m. we stand on doorsteps to clap.
Fireworks are launched into daylight.
With the bell of a saucepan, the lady across the road
fills the sky with birds. They circle, then settle, nearer.

When I wake, it is the heat of stepping off a plane.
Sleep is another country I rush to enter.

I didn't send Grandad a birthday card. I was told
the spit I used to seal the envelope might kill him.

Round 21: Geography
My bedroom is 25 hand widths wide, 42 long.

I give my afternoons to the patch of wall to the left
of my computer screen, where two textures
of wallpaper meet under whitewash.

I am forbidden to prop open the fire door.

I try yoga. I don't hoover.

I mistake 'wander' for 'wonder' so my answers
are always wrong.

Round 17: Food and drink
I cut my hair with kitchen scissors.
Hair peppers my meals.

I climb out onto the roof to share nachos
and guacamole with the crow.

Round 42: Pictures
My table is a gappy jigsaw of dog breeds, a pile of eyes
saved for last.

I press my forehead against the window so that I cannot see
the frame. A new item in the skip today
– a toilet seat, lid open like wings.

Canesten 500mg Pessary

I half expect it to rattle the moment I pop the applicator and the little white tablet settles on the wall of my vagina. Every month the girl behind the counter tells me to do it at night (cleaner, that way), and in return I hurry her with a lie about a diagnosis of thrush, hand her the tenner and walk home with the box under my arm. I take a stinging piss, sink into duvet and let the streetlight find its way through the gap between blind and window to yellow my thighs. For three days I quietly fizz. My pessaries dissolve to the movement of the 43 bus, to the cross-legged clapping at the theatre, to the strides up Park Street stunted by pencil skirt. I put one up me 35,997 feet above sea level and when I landed in India I hand-washed clothes in a blue bucket and thumbnail-scraped white paste off my pants. I'd have a white bouquet of applicators if I collected them all. My pessaries are proof. They come after long weekends of effervescence, of pints on King Street, of drinking coffee when thirsty, of climbing into the stranger of each other.

Accounting

In this year I am copywriter, I am poet. I am full-time for someone else and full-time for myself.

In this year I moved house in a heatwave. I moved for a garden but the garden is paved. Desperate to catch and keep the rain I pushed cereal bowls under honeysuckle, plunged thirsty lupins into stew pots. I pressed poet into paint bucket, thumbed copywriter into upturned dustbin lid. I angle myself towards clouds and wait.

In this year the days slid down the wall. The flies spoke back. The bins overflowed and the seagulls watched our undoing from the safety of scaffolding. A silhouette of a woman on the crest of the hill emptied her pockets for crows.

In this year copywriter slid down the wall. Poet spoke back. To give the day an end I bundle myself into the bath like bad fruit. I give my Sundays to the patch of wall to the left of my pillow. I bundle copywriter into the bath like bad poet.

In this year I talk in circles. My mouth has forgotten the shape of no. My skin is too close to my body. I pray for rain as though I could hide things in the dull mirrors of it. In the tight view from a city window a silhouette of a copywriter on the crest of the hill empties her poet for crows.

Meeting After a Break-Up to Discuss Outstanding Utility Bills

I watch you peel an orange
so precisely that the skin remains intact
and holds the shape of what was once in it.
The pores burst into the light, fall on me in a mist.

I watch you pick the pith from under your nails
by scraping them on your teeth.
I expect to smell orange peel whenever I raise
a hand to my mouth to stifle
a yawn, or a scream.

Lethelane

n.: the feeling of visiting a place for the final time

I have met you three times, Lethelane.
Once in a piazza in Amalfi,
shading under a clock, espresso at my lip.
Once at the pond my dad dug,
a graveyard for broken toys.
Once in X's lounge with a sofa
too big for the room, like a swollen tongue.

I breathed in the coffee, the mud, the rug
and you arrived, Lethelane, claws first.
Your talons pierced my stomach,
you spread your slate-black feathers
around my abdomen.

I hope to never meet you again, Lethelane,
but hear you scrape the ground,
sharpening, behind me.

Celandine

I enter the woodland as if tomorrow
had pushed me. The wind shushed

through the newest green of wild garlic
and there, under a canopy of hazel and birch,

a floor laced in bright yellow stars,
each bursting with ten narrow petals.

Rich in vitamin C yet toxic when eaten
I want so much to sink into them,

to swim in their yellow, kick out
and breaststroke through thick light.

They predict the weather, the swallows'
return, their petals open at good news.

I spend the afternoon down at the river,
return to the woodland on my way home

to find the yellow petals closing with the sun.
I wait for every flower to shut into thousands

of flutes, each becomes a second I am older,
a moment I have grown with this wood.

Jam Toast

On screen, Lucy pushes her way
through fur to the back of a backless
wardrobe into a century-long winter.
Is Narnia real? asks my niece.
Can we check Nanny's cupboard?

Beside her, my five-year-old nephew licks
his palm, uninterested in the narrative
on second viewing, the remote next to him
longer than his thigh. *It's not real*, he says,
because you can start it again.

Left-Handed

There's something other-dimensional about watching you write with your left hand, something uneasy, like walking to the back of a bus as it pulls forward. Perhaps I'm jealous of the way you give yourself wholly to the page. Your wrist, then forearm, wipe out each word as you set it down. Revision is not a luxury your body allows you. I crave this irrevocability, the freedom in being blind to your last word. I tried it once. I fumbled through a sentence with my left hand, barely keeping the end of each vowel from drowning under the line. I chose the wrong pen. The ink didn't have time to dry before my arm erased its intention and smeared each letter into the next like days in a quick week. Like a grey secret. I walked to the sink with the black trail down my arm, ran the tap, the cold residue of words dripping from my elbow onto the white porcelain.

Trevose Head Lighthouse

When the storm blackened our windows
we buried ourselves

in cotton and each other and began to build
the weather in a jigsaw.

First, the corners to set our boundary, then
to find spring in one thousand pieces.

The lighthouse took shape from gappy fog
in the window on the floor.

We stuffed rockpools with clouds and birds
in flight and, pleased with our efforts,

placed the confetti-blossom in the gutter.
Our foreground bodied out.

In the light of the season of this room
we warmed our hands, subtracted a layer

from each other and moved on all fours
in search of the last piece of sky.

What counts as haunting?

I'm asking for a woman in a white coat

When you're young they don't tell you you'll be opening
    and closing windows until you don't

When they say *someone just walked over my grave*
    they mean someone only a river away

My niece thinks we carry the dead on our backs
    and when I consider this, I see a rucksack left open

In a game of hide-and-seek reworded as organ donation
    a heart can swap bodies

I walk in rush hour in case I brush past that second body

Heaven might be shit and no one's said whether ghosts
    have ghosts who have ghosts

Someone is having the same dream I had for weeks
    the one where I fall in love with the man who received
    your donated heart and my future daughter holds up her
    foot to tie her laces, asks, *what does it feel like to be buried?*

I answer, *ask your father when he picks you up from school*

Venice

A boat's mast passes among chimneys. A man bobs at a floating bus stop. The tower leans to hear the water telling it of its thirst for the rooftops. There are no pigeons in Piazza San Marco. Perhaps they let a bird of prey circle the first Tuesday of every month to scare them off. I stand in-between the two string bands on either side of the square. I wait for afternoon to touch the gold tiling of the basilica. I wait for it to appear as if in flames and burn ferociously on the violin's wail.

@HumanForScale

At lunch I scroll past an ichthyosaur – a sea-dragon fossil
found in Rutland. A woman sits, calf-like, in its dug outline.

Under my thumb a teenager is lying on a plastic sheet:
Triceratops femur vs elephant femur vs me. Fun lab break!

Mostly the humans are smiling or at least showing teeth.
My thumb stops at a woman whose body has replaced half

a whale's skull. Her stiff existence half of a two-pronged
fork. Her arms crossed over her chest, eyes shut to the sun

baking the bones. The whale's eyes full of bracken, grass.
This woman was hiding her teeth, her face doggedly dead,

accepting herself as skeleton too under the blue of her jeans
– beached, waiting with the whale for the water to rise.

Not Yet Walking

My niece stands clinging to the furniture,
a light wobble on the tightrope of her feet.
She moves, branch to branch, table leg to sofa,
carefully tracing the outline of the house
as if gathering for the day she's left with nothing.

You could have been her uncle
but, instead, you left me to trace
the white chalk outline of our years together.
You could have been her uncle.

I kiss her like I'm starving.
I wonder when she'll know that my mouth
coming towards her endlessly is a good thing.

You could have been her uncle
but, instead, you stood in the centre of the room
where my niece and I couldn't reach,
and we were left to figure out
the relationship between
foot and ground, ground and foot.

Is my rain the same rain as yours?

Rain is only rain for a handful of minutes,
its entire existence is the falling, then
it's a puddle, wet hair, wetter tongue,
a drain clogged with winter.

Tower blocks reach to catch rain sooner.
I imagine it falling through the building,
shower by shower, glasses of water, the wetting
of toothbrushes in a week-long timelapse.

I stir awake to the neighbour's blender breaking
down solids until they're defined as wet.
Rain runs down my window and collects street-
light with it. As it falls, I move downstairs, upstairs,
then down again and it's still falling.

I am still myself when I reach the ground.
One time my kitchen tap ran brown so I let it
pour. It was the earth pushing itself up to meet
rain at the height of conversation.

Ghazal for when I think of you,
I think of me

It's been enough years since burying you that my grief has turned
180° to face my face instead. Here is a secret spoken in gravefuls.

Five past the rowan is your headstone – an open book with blank page.
Reflected in its granite: wipe of a bird, conifers leaning to read your grave.

There is no afterlife, but you arrived at your funeral without a heart,
lungs, pancreas, kidneys or liver. Your body will have seven other gravelets.

In thick cathedral light, the loudest hymn was the creak of wicker coffin.
What is singing if not the mouth being the body's own gravedigger?

I've been asked what I will write about next. I am scared I need your death.
If I laid out all my poems on the wet ground, they'd be mistaken for graves.

Joyce's Pool, January 4th

A source of the Bristol River Avon

I step-stalk down the bank
to the frozen surface of this scraggy
spring at the edge of the A433.
An unassuming body of water
named after a girl who drowned
looking for herself.

There is an exposure that comes
with frost – it makes the world
more known with every step,
each layer of fallen alder, ash
and oak leaf crisp-shushes, snaps.

With every collapse, I am almost
sorry. With each hollow I fill,
I learn a new vowel.
I crouch to peer into the pool's
glass case of winter; a dragonfly larva,
belly-up, clinging to the under-ice,
the warning-red of a berry,
a curled O of blonde fibre.

At the pool's centre, air bubbles
are trapped, as big as plates.

In their crown shyness, the trees
dome over the pool but do not touch.
Their branches hold eddies of sky.
Catkins reach for the underworld
below this pool's opening.
I press my hand to the ice
until it stings, then push.

In the same sound – the ice cracks,
water rushes to soothe over
the broken lip. I know why
I have come here:

        to witness a beginning
        to see it shattered
        to see it remake itself
        to begin again

Acknowledgements

My gratitude goes to the editors of the following journals, magazines and projects, where versions of some of these poems appeared: *Anthropocene*, *Banshee*, *Dust*, *The Great Margin*, *Ink, Sweat and Tears*, *The Interpreter's House*, *Magma*, *The Moth*, *Neon* (who published 'Three-Second Storm' and 'On Pigeons,' which they kindly nominated for the Forward Prize), *Propel*, *The Rialto*, *Steel Jackdaw*, *Under the Radar*.

Thanks to Paper Nations, Tracy Harris and Tom Gatley for making 'Trevose Head Lighthouse' into a poetry film.

'Accounting' was commissioned by musician Ru Brooks, producer of Revaux, for *Swells*, an Arts Council-funded poetry soundscape of artists who were asked to write about the experience of their creative practice in lockdown.

'Index of Exeter Quay/From the blue door, I beckon' was commissioned by Literature Works as part of my writer-in-residence position at Exeter Custom House for Quay Words.

'Notes addressed to the person who received my ex's heart' was awarded second place in the Magma Poetry Competition in 2022.

'Notes on Hung Road' and 'Three-Second Storm' were written while poet-in-residence for Boat Poets, an Arts Council-funded project which encourages young people to connect with their local river.

'Notes on Hung Road' won the Brian Dempsey Memorial Prize for Best Single Poem 2021. That, and 'Typographer in the basement', were published in Dempsey & Windle's anthology *Horses of a different colour.*

'Outfitting a Kayak' was awarded second place in Black Eyes Publishing and Gloucester Poetry Society's Open Poetry Competition 2021.

Thanks

To my agent Becky Thomas at Lewinsohn Literary for opening this journey by emailing me: *Shall we venture forth?*

To my publisher, Sarah Castleton, for such tender guidance and support. I am so very happy this book found you.

To Martha Sprackland for copyediting this collection with such clarity, concision and rigour.

To my teachers Andy Brown, Patricia Wallace and Tim Liardet.

To my MA team Josie Alford and Nicola Heaney. I did the book! Pint soon?

To my trusty poetry critique groups HOURS and Bristol Stanza.

To Caleb Parkin, for all the last-minute feedback pleas and poem swaps.

To Society of Authors and Authors' Foundation for the John Brooks Award for authors based in the West Country.

To the Jewish Literary Foundation for awarding me a place on their first Genesis Emerging Writers programme and to George Szirtes for his mentorship.

To Nina, for being beside me at the funeral.

To Lou, for our sisterhood, for reading the early poems in bed with me.

To the Ince family.

To Globe360, for teaching me how to scull.

To my beloved Exeter girls, Bethan, Bridie, Gen and Izzy – for becoming women together.

To my family – I was writing this acknowledgement long before the first poem. How lucky I am to know such love. This book is made of you. Squillions, Socks x

To Lil – Thank you for proofing every email and pulling me through every glitch. I adore rattling around with you in our sweet little life.

To River Avon, for its holding.

RAISING READERS
Books Build Bright Futures

Dear Reader,

We'd love your attention for one more page to tell you about the crisis in children's reading, and what we can all do.

Studies have shown that reading for fun is the **single biggest predictor of a child's future life chances** – more than family circumstance, parents' educational background or income. It improves academic results, mental health, wealth, communication skills, ambition and happiness.[1]

The number of children reading for fun is in rapid decline. Young people have a lot of competition for their time. In 2024, 1 in 10 children and young people in the UK aged 5 to 18 did not own a single book at home.[2]

Hachette works extensively with schools, libraries and literacy charities, but here are some ways we can all raise more readers:

- Reading to children for just 10 minutes a day makes a difference
- Don't give up if children aren't regular readers – there will be books for them!
- Visit bookshops and libraries to get recommendations
- Encourage them to listen to audiobooks
- Support school libraries
- Give books as gifts

There's a lot more information about how to encourage children to read on our website: **www.RaisingReaders.co.uk**

Thank you for reading.

hachette
UK

[1] OECD, '21st-Century Readers: Developing Literacy Skills in a Digital World', 2021, https://www.oecd.org/en/publications/21st-century-readers_a83d84cb-en.html

[2] National Literacy Trust, 'Book Ownership in 2024', November 2024, https://literacytrust.org.uk/research-services/research-reports/book-ownership-in-2024

First Nations and Native American Cookbook

Second Edition

By Tim Murphy

Copyright 2016
Shamrock Arrow Media

For information on Flannel John's
Cookbooks visit www.flanneljohn.com

First Nations
and
Native American
Cookbook

TABLE OF CONTENTS

RECIPES

ACORN CAKES
(Apache)

  1 cup of acorn meal
  1 cup of cornmeal
  Water
  ¼ cup of Honey
  1 tablespoon of oil or melted butter
  Pinch of salt

Mix the ingredients with enough warm water to make a moist dough but not sticky. Divide the dough into 12 balls. Cover and let the dough rest for 10 minutes or until ready to use. Lightly moisten your hands with water and pat the balls into thick tortillas. Heat an ungreased cast iron skillet on medium high heat. Place the cakes in the skillet. Cook until the edges start to get dry. Lift the cake a little with a spatula to check for doneness. When done, flip over and cook the other side. When both sides are slightly brown they are done.

ARCTIC CHAR
(Inuit)

1 pound of arctic char fillets
1 onion, sliced into rings
Pepper, fresh ground if possible

Bring a grill or campfire up to medium heat. Lightly oil the grill or grate. Place the fish on a piece of aluminum foil. Please the onion rings on top and pepper to taste. Wrap foil around the fish but do not seal the top. Place the fish in the foil on a grill and close the cover. If cooking in the open air, tent another piece of foil over the fish. Cook for 15 minutes or until fish flakes easily with a fork.

BAKED PUMPKIN
(Ojibwa)

1 small pumpkin
¼ cup of maple syrup
¼ cup of apple cider
¼ cup of melted butter

Place the pumpkin in an oven and bake at 350 degrees
for 90 minutes to 2 hours. Cut a hole in the top and
scoop out the seeds and the pulp. Set seeds aside for
later snacking. Mix together the maple syrup, apple
cider and butter thoroughly. Pour into the pumpkin and
bake for 35 minutes. Cut into wedges and serve.